MAKE ME LAUGH AGAIN

100 Animal Jokes

100 Monster Jokes

100 Knock Knock Jokes

Copyright© 1982, 1984 by Lerner Publication Company
Published by Price/Stern/Sloan Publishers, Inc.
410 North La Cienega Boulevard, Los Angeles, California 90048

ISBN: 0-8431-1007-4

MAKE ME
LAUGH AGAIN

100 Animal Jokes

100 Monster Jokes

100 Knock Knock Jokes

By Sam Schultz

Illustrated by Joan Hanson

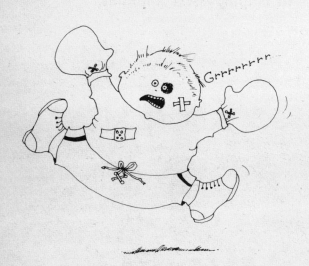

PRICE/STERN/SLOAN
Publishers, Inc., Los Angeles
1984

Harry: I have a pet mouse that squeaks all day.
Larry: Why don't you try oiling it?

Q: Why does your pet owl go "Tweet, tweet"?
A: Because it doesn't give a hoot!

Kerry: We just sold our thoroughbred horse
for one hundred dollars.
Sherry: We just sold our thoroughbred
fox terrier.
Kerry: What did you sell it for?
Sherry: For wetting on the carpet!

Q: What's big and red and hides behind a tree?
A: An embarrassed elephant.

Q: What can a cat have that dogs can't have?
A: Kittens.

Two fleas came out of a movie theater. They saw it was raining outside. One flea said to the other, "Do you want to walk, or should we take a dog?"

Lady Customer: I'd like a pair of alligator shoes.
Salesman: Of course, miss. What size is your alligator?

Q: How can you keep a goat from smelling?
A: Cut off its nose!

Eye Doctor: What seems to be the trouble?
Leopard Trainer: I don't know. I keep seeing spots before my eyes!

Q: Why are elephants ashamed to go to the beach?
A: Because they have a hard time keeping their trunks up!

Mark: My dog sleeps with me at night.
Susie: Ugh, that's not healthy!
Mark: I know, but he doesn't mind.

Q: What can an elephant have that a flea
can't have?
A: An elephant can have fleas, but a flea
can't have elephants!

Q: What should you do when a bull charges you?
A: Pay him!

First Dog: My master calls me "Tootsie."
What does your master call you?
Second Dog: He calls me "Sitboy"!

Father Kangaroo: Why are you spanking Junior?
Mother Kangaroo: Because he's been eating
crackers in bed.

Q: What side of a cat has the most fur?
A: The outside.

Ron: A bear ran through our camp last week, and our camp leader shot the bear in his pajamas.
Don: Don't kid me. Bears don't wear pajamas!

First Snake: I sure hope I'm not poisonous!
Second Snake: Why?
First Snake: Because I just bit my tongue!

Q: Why does your dog always scratch himself in the same spot?
A: Because that's where he itches!

Q: Who do you feel more sorry for—a dog or a cat?
A: A cat. Because cats are such purr things.

Q: What do dogs and trees have in common?
A: Their bark.

Dick: Hey, your dog just bit my ankle.
Rick: What did you expect? He's just a small dog, and he can't reach any higher!

Rodney: Did you know an elephant never forgets?
Irving: Big deal! What does he have to remember?

Q: When is the best time to take your pet lion for a walk?
A: Any time he wants to go!

Jack: My dog is worth $500.00.
Mack: How can a dog save that much money?

Tiger Cub: Look Mom, I'm chasing a hunter around a tree!

Mother Tiger: How many times must I tell you not to play with your food?

Hy: If I say, "Come here, Rover," will your dog come to me?

Sy: Nope.

Hy: Why not?

Sy: Because his name's Fido!

Teacher: Susie, name four members of the cat family.

Susie: Mother, father, sister, and brother.

Little Worm: Am I late, Mother?

Mother Worm: Yes! Where in earth have you been?

Veterinarian: Has your cat ever had any fleas?

Cat Owner: No, just kittens.

Dan: My parents just bought me a bird for a pet.
Jan: What kind is it?
Dan: A keet.
Jan: You mean a parakeet.
Dan: No, they only bought me one.

Q: What was the elephant doing on the freeway?
A: About five miles per hour!

Hank: I took my dog to a movie yesterday,
    but he didn't want to stay.
Frank: Why not?
Hank: He thought the book was better!

Q: What did one old firefly say to the other?
A: "Your grandson sure is bright for his age!"

Marty: My mother can't stand my pet duck.
Arty: Why not?
Marty: He's a wise quacker.

Mr. Johnson: I can't get my police dog to open his mouth. You'd better get over here quick!

Policeman: Mister, you don't want the police. You want a veterinarian.

Mr. Johnson: No, I want the police. I can't get him to open his mouth because he has a burglar in it!

Billy: I just bought five ducks and five pounds of cheese.

Willy: What for?

Billy: Because I like cheese and quackers!

Dick: What happened to you?

Pam: I fell while I was riding.

Dick: Horseback?

Pam: I don't know. I'll find out when I get back to the stable!

Q: What do you get when an elephant bumps into a cherry tree?

A: A cherry shake!

Q: Why do elephants travel in groups?

A: Because group rates are cheaper!

Q: Why is a dog man's best friend?
A: Because he wags his tail instead of his tongue.

Arnie: My dog tried to arrest me for crossing the street against the light.
Annie: You mean he tried to stop you from crossing the street.
Arnie: No, he tried to arrest me. He's a police dog.

Q: What kind of dog would a person bite?
A: A hot dog!

Jimmy: I've got a pet pig named Ball Point.
Timmy: Ball Point? That's a funny name for a pig.
Jimmy: That's his pen name.

Q: Why didn't the owners of a lost dog advertise for him in the paper?
A: Because the dog couldn't read.

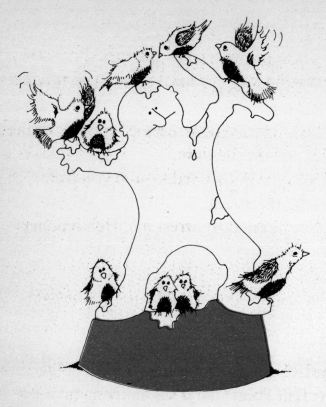

Teacher: If this statue came to life, what do you think it would say?
Student: "Anybody want a pet pigeon?"

Peter: I've got a cat who can say its own name!
Karen: That's great! What's your cat's name?
Peter: "Meow."

Polly: How do you know ants are smart?
Molly: Because they always seem to know when we're having a picnic.

Mother: Willy, I thought I told you not to teach your parrot any bad words!
Willy: I'm not, Mom. I'm just telling him what he's not supposed to say!

Q: Why do cats look larger at night than in the morning?
A: Because they're usually let out at night and taken in in the morning.

Woman: When you sold me this cat you promised me it would be good for mice.

Clerk: Isn't it?

Woman: It hasn't caught a mouse since I've had it.

Clerk: Isn't that good for mice?

Q: What would you get if you'd cross a canary with a cat?

A: A peeping tom.

Teacher: How do you spell leopard?

Student: L-E-P-A-R-D.

Teacher: The dictionary spells it L-E-O-P-A-R-D.

Student: But you asked me how *I* spell it!

Q: What kind of dog hands out tickets?

A: A police dog.

Q: What kind of sharks never eat women?

A: Man-eating sharks!

Mother: Billy, why did you pull the cat's tail?
Billy: I didn't pull his tail, Mother. I was standing on it, and *he* pulled it.

Will: I've got an alligator named Ginger.
Jill: Does Ginger bite?
Will: No, Ginger snaps.

First Leopard: Well, how did you enjoy dinner?
Second Leopard: It sure hit the spots!

First Cow: I just can't get over what I saw last night.
Second Cow: What was it?
First Cow: The moon.

Cat: My master gets a kick out of me.
Dog: When my master tries that, he gets a bite out of me!

Game Warden: Young man, it's against the law to fish in this lake!

Young Man: Oh, I'm not fishing, sir. I'm just teaching my pet worm how to swim!

Q: Why do elephants always have wrinkles?
A: Because they're too big to iron out.

Q: Why can't rabbits go bald?
A: Because they keep producing hares.

Two kangaroos were walking through the park. One kangaroo asked the other where her son was. She looked down at her empty pouch and screamed, "Help! My pocket's been picked!"

Q: Why does your cat make such an awful noise at night?
A: Ever since she ate the canary she thinks she can sing!

Mother: Why are you crying?
Little Girl: Because I wanted to get a dog for my new baby brother.
Mother: Well, that's no reason to cry.
Little Girl: Yes it is! Nobody would trade me!

Q: What kind of cat hangs around a bowling alley?
A: An alley cat.

Q: Why did the elephant quit the circus?
A: He didn't want to work for peanuts anymore.

Q: Why do hummingbirds hum?
A: Because they don't know the words!

Mrs. Jones: Why does your son always say, "Cluck, cluck, cluck"?
Mrs. Smith: Because he thinks he's a chicken.
Mrs. Jones: Why don't you tell him he's not a chicken?
Mrs. Smith: Because we need the eggs!

Georgie: Yesterday I came face to face with a lion!

Porgie: Weren't you scared?

Georgie: Naw. I just turned away and walked past his cage.

Q: Why don't animals make good dancers?

A: Because they have two left feet!

Jack: I'd like some bird seed, please.

Pet Store Clerk: How many birds do you have?

Jack: None. I want to grow some!

Q: Why did the farmer put bells on his cow?

A: Because the horns didn't work.

Q: Why did the man count elephants in his sleep instead of sheep?

A: Because he was nearsighted.

Q: What sounds worse than a cat up a tree?
A: Two cats up a tree.

Barry: We have a new dog!
Bessie: What's he like?
Barry: Anything we feed him!

Q: What is cow hide used for?
A: To hold the cow together.

Q: What did the mother skunk tell her son after she gave him a chemistry set?
A: "Now don't smell up the house."

First Boy: I can't talk to you while my goat is nearby.
Second Boy: Why not?
First Boy: Because he always butts in.

Billy: I just saw a man-eating shark.
Willy: Where?
Billy: In a restaurant!

Q: What does a skunk do when it's angry?
A: Raises a stink.

Betsy: I'd like some booties for my dog's birthday.
Store Clerk: You'll have to bring your dog in to try some on.
Betsy: I can't do that! I want them to be a surprise.

Q: How do you get down from an elephant?
A: You don't. You get down from a goose.

Q: What did the boy say when his cat began to purr?
A: "He left his motor running!"

Pet Store Owner: Yes, I have a singing cat and
　mouse for sale.
Buyer: Do they really sing?
Pet Store Owner: Well, to tell you the truth,
　the cat is a ventriloquist!

Davy: My dog ate my reading book.
Sally: What did you do about it?
Davy: I took the words right out of his mouth.

Joey: My dog Ossie is sick, so we're taking him
　to an animal doctor.
Moey: Gee, I thought all doctors were people!

A man ran over Mrs. Smith's cat. He went to her
　door to apologize.
Man: I would like to replace your cat.
Mrs. Smith: Well, you'd better do it fast. There's
　a mouse in the kitchen!

Q: What does a rabbit use to comb its fur?
A: A harebrush.

Boy: How much are those puppies in the window?

Pet Store Man: Twenty dollars apiece.

Boy: How much is a whole one?

Dick: I taught my dog to play checkers.

Joe: Really? You must have a pretty smart dog.

Dick: Not that smart. I can beat him two out of three games!

Q: How many elephants can you fit in a Volkswagen?

A: Five. Two in front, two in back, and one in the glove compartment!

Q: What kind of snake snaps at people?

A: A garter snake.

Mailman: Your dog bit my leg!

Woman: Did you put anything on it?

Mailman: No, he seemed to like it just the way it was.

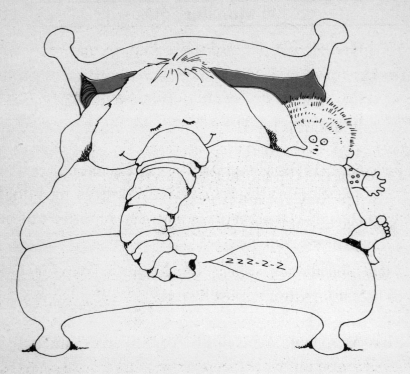

Q: Why do puppies make better pets than elephants?

A: Try taking an elephant to bed with you and you'll soon find out!

Q: What's the difference between an elephant and a mouse?

A: About 5,000 pounds.

Jack: I got a cow for my birthday.
Jane: Does it give milk?
Jack: No, I have to take it from her.

Q: How would you know if there's an elephant under your bed when you wake up from your sleep?

A: Your nose would be touching the ceiling.

Q: What did the man say when his dog ran away?
A: Doggone-it!

Q: How do you tell a good monster from a bad one?
A: If you meet a good monster, you'll be able to talk about it later!

Q: What did the mother ghost say to her son when they got into the car?
A: Be sure to fasten your sheet belt.

Ad in monster newspaper: "Use Mummy Soap for that School-Ghoul complexion."

First Astronaut: What has 6 eyes, 10 arms, and is green all over?
Second Astronaut: I don't know.
First Astronaut: I don't know, either, but it's looking in our window!

Q: Where would you find a one-handed monster?
A: In a second-hand store.

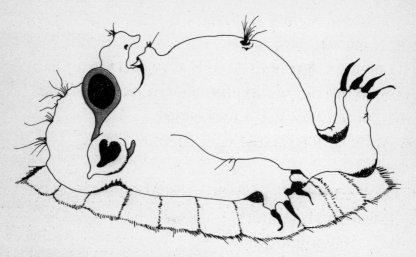

Q: What do you do with a green monster?
A: Put it in the sun until it ripens.

Q: Did you hear about the vampire's coffin?
A: He stopped after he took a cough drop.

A monster agreed to go to Hollywood to star in a movie when the director offered him a role he could *really* sink his teeth into!

Q: What do you get when you cross a monster with a computer?
A: A 500-pound genius.

Q: What kind of banks do vampires go to?
A: Blood banks.

Q: Did you hear about the vampire's coffin?
A: He stopped after he took a cough drop.

A monster agreed to go to Hollywood to star in a movie when the director offered him a role he could *really* sink his teeth into!

Q: What do you get when you cross a monster with a computer?
A: A 500-pound genius.

Q: What kind of banks do vampires go to?
A: Blood banks.

Q: How do you greet a three-headed monster?
A: Hello! Hello! Hello! How are you? How are you? How are you?

Q: Why was the monster afraid to leave his house?

A: He didn't like what he read in his horror-scope.

Child Monster: Mama, I have a stomachache.
Mother Monster: It must be someone you ate.

Witch Hazel: Wilma, did you put the cat out?
Witch Wilma: Why, is it on fire?

Q: Pretend you're surrounded by 50 werewolves and 30 vampires. What would you do?
A: I'd stop pretending!

First Monster: I'm starved!
Second Monster: Dinner is thawing in the refrigerator.
First Monster: Oh good. Who is it?

Q: Who would name a monster King Tut?
A: His mummy.

First Monster: Am I late for dinner?
Second Monster: Yes, everyone's been eaten.

Q: Did you hear about the football game
between the Dallas Cowboys and a team of
monsters?
A: Yeah, the Cowboys were eaten alive!

A fiery dragon captured a knight in armor.
The knight begged the dragon to be kind to him
because he hadn't had a bite in three days.
So the dragon bit him!

Q: What steps would you take if a monster was
about to attack you?
A: Long ones!

Q: What happened to the monster that ate the electric company?
A: He was in shock for a week.

Q: Why don't monsters cross the road?
A: Because they don't want to be mistaken for chickens.

Q: By which lake is there a monster motel?
A: Lake Erie.

First Monster: What's this we're eating?
Second Monster: Ladyfingers.
First Monster: They're delicious. I hope the rest of the lady tastes this good!

Q: Why do witches fly around on broomsticks?
A: Because they're cheaper than airplanes.

Q: What did the vampire catch after staying up all night?

A: A bat cold.

Young Frankenstein's monstrous invention
Caused trouble too awful to mention.
His actions were ghoulish
Which proves it is foolish
To monkey with Nature's intention!

Q: What's the best thing to do if you meet a blue monster?

A: Cheer him up.

Q: What did the monster say to his blind date?

A: You look good enough to eat.

Q: Did you hear about the cookie monster who almost drowned?

A: He tried to dunk himself in a vat of milk.

First Monster: You mean you went to college, but you *still* eat your victims?

Second Monster: Yes, but now I use a knife and a fork!

Q: Why did the monster fall in love with a piano?

A: Because it had such beautiful straight teeth.

Sheriff: Did you see a monster take this road a short time ago?

Young Man: No, the road is still here.

Q: Did you hear the new Werewolf band last Saturday?

A: Yes, it was a howling success.

Mary Monster: George is a real dummy.

Alice Monster: Why do you say that?

Mary Monster: He can't count to 40 without taking his shoes off!

A monster adrift on a raft
Had never been on such a craft.
He fashioned a sail
With his body and tail
While the fishes around him just laughed.

Q: What do you call a monster who ate his
mother's sister?
A: An aunt-eater.

Knight Teacher: How can you keep a dragon
from charging?
Knight Student: By taking away his credit card.

Q: What's green, weighs 2,000 pounds, and has
8 wheels?
A: A monster on roller skates.

Joe: What's the difference between a monster
and a watermelon?
Moe: I don't know.
Joe: Well, then I'll never send *you* to the store
for a watermelon!

Q: What do you get when you cross a monster with a parrot?

A: I don't know. But when it talks, you'd better listen!

First Vampire: I called the gang and told them we're playing cards at the cemetery tonight.

Second Vampire: Why there?

First Vampire: Well, if someone doesn't show, we can always dig up another player.

Q: What's big and mean and only eats candy rocks?

A: The Big Rock Candy Monster.

Q: Did you hear about the monster rock band?

A: They played to screaming audiences every night!

Q: What's the best way to approach an evil-eyed monster?

A: *Very* carefully!

Q: Why didn't the vampire want to play baseball?
A: Because he didn't want to damage his bats.

Q: What must a ghost buy before he can scare anyone?
A: A haunting license.

Girl Monster: You must think I'm a perfect idiot.
Boy Monster: No, of course not. Nobody's perfect!

A fire-breathing monster in Spain
Woke up with a terrible pain.
It wasn't his dream
That caused him to scream,
But he had set his huge tail aflame!

Tim: Why do monsters have square shoulders?
Jim: Because they eat lots of cereal.
Tim: How can cereal give them square shoulders?
Jim: It's not the cereal. It's the boxes!

Monster mother to child: I told you never to speak with someone in your mouth!

First Vampire: You're a pain in the neck.
Second Vampire: Thank you for the compliment!

Q: Why doesn't Dracula trust the Invisible Man?
A: Because he can see right through him.

Mother Cannibal: Junior was sent home from school today.
Father Cannibal: Why, what did he do?
Mother Cannibal: He tried to butter up his teacher!

First Monster: You don't have a brain in your head.
Second Monster: Which head?

Two sea monsters had just finished eating a fisherman. "You know," said one to the other, "I'd like fishermen a lot better if they didn't have so many bones."

Child Monster: Mama, may I eat New York City?
Mother Monster: Only if you wash your hands first.

Q: Why did the vampire call the morgue?
A: He wanted to see if they delivered.

Q: Did you hear about the new vampire delivery service?
A: It's a fly-by-night operation!

Lou: Never play catch with a 5,000-pound monster.
Sue: Why not?
Lou: Because they're very, very heavy!

Q: Did you hear about the bald-headed man who met a man-eating monster?
A: He had a hair-raising experience!

Don: Three monsters were arrested for throwing a party.
Ron: Why?
Don: They threw it across the Grand Canyon!

Q: Why did the monster cross the road?
A: To eat the chicken.

First Monster: A nice family moved next door to me.
Second Monster: I hope they'll be people you can enjoy.
First Monster: Enjoy? I think they'll be *delicious!*

Q: Why did the vampires ask a ghost to join their football team?
A: Because they needed some team spirit.

Q: Where did the witch keep her flying machine?
A: In the br-r-r-oom closet.

Q: What's the best way to talk to a people-eating monster?
A: By long distance!

Tommy Ghost: Mother, can I join the army?
Mother Ghost: No, but you can join the Ghost Guard.

First Monster: Where are you going?
Second Monster: I'm going to school.
First Monster: Why don't you take a bus?
Second Monster: Nah. My mom will only make me take it back.

Q: What do sea monsters eat for dinner?
A: Fish and ships.

Q: Do vampires have holidays?
A: Sure, haven't you ever heard of Fangsgiving Day?

Q: Why did the little girl monster eat a box of bullets?
A: She wanted to grow bangs.

Mother Monster: Do you think we should take Junior to the zoo?
Father Monster: Certainly not! If the zoo wants Junior, they can come and get him!

Q: What does Dracula do when the sun comes up?
A: He takes a coffin break.

A giant green monster from Blister
Decided to eat up his sister
And when he was through
He cried, "What did I do?"
Now he's sorry he did, 'cause he missed her.

Mother Monster: Son, I thought I told you to drink your medicine after your hot bath.

Son Monster: I'm sorry, Mom. But after I finished drinking the bath I couldn't drink another drop!

Monster Doctor: What seems to be the trouble?

Monster Patient: I don't know. I feel upset.

Monster Doctor: Well, maybe you're just fed up with people.

Q: What's red and white on the outside, and green and lumpy on the inside?

A: A can of Cream of Monster soup.

Mother monster to child: How many times must I tell you to play with your food before you eat it?

Did you hear about the monster who rented a hotel room and ate the mattress?

A: The sign in front of the hotel said, "Bed and Breakfast."

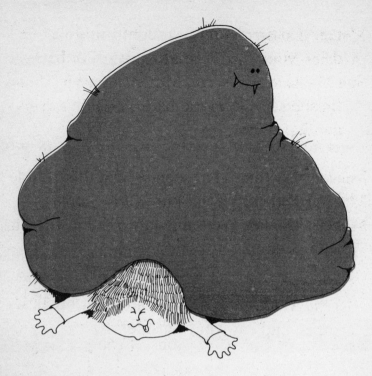

Q: What's a monster's favorite sport?
A: Squash.

A brave knight carefully planned how he would slay the fire-breathing dragon and then marry the king's daughter. But when he finally found the dragon, all his plans went up in smoke!

Q: Did you hear about the monster that ate China?
A: He was hungry an hour later!

First Monster: We must be in a city.
Second Monster: What makes you think so?
First Monster: We're stepping on more people!

Q: What do you call a city that monsters live in?
A: A monstrosity (Monstro-city).

Child Monster: Here's a present for you.
Mother Monster: Thank you. It's beautiful.
Child Monster: I made it with my own ten hands!

Secretary: Mr. Jones, the Invisible Man is here to see you.
Mr. Jones: Tell him I can't possibly see him.

First Monster: (After catching an airplane in flight) How do you eat one of these things?
Second Monster: Like a peanut. Just break it open and eat what's inside!

Q: Why do dragons sleep in the daytime?
A: So they can hunt knights.

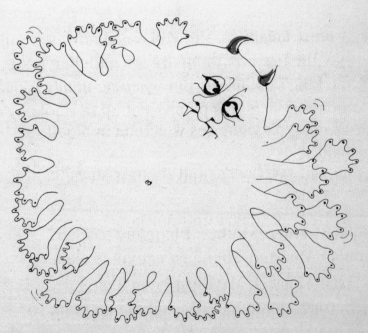

Mary: I just saw a monster with 60 arms, and I didn't even run.
Gary: Weren't you scared?
Mary: Nah! He didn't have a leg to stand on!

Q: What do monsters have that no one else can
have?
A: Baby monsters!

Q: What kind of werewolves never need
ironing?
A: Wash and werewolves.

Q: Why aren't vampires welcome in blood
banks?
A: Because they only make withdrawals.

Child Monster: Mother, I hate my teacher.
Mother Monster: Then just eat your salad.

Dan: Why did the monster paint his toes red?
Jan: I don't know. Why?
Dan: So he could hide in a cherry tree.
Jan: I've never seen a monster in a cherry tree.
Dan: See? It works!

Knock, Knock.   Who's there?
Annie.   Annie, who?
Annie body home?

Knock, Knock.   Who's there?
Boo.   Boo, who?
What are you crying about?

Knock, Knock.   Who's there?
Ya.   Ya, who?
I didn't know you'd be so glad to see me!

Knock, Knock.   Who's there?
Ben.   Ben, who?
Ben looking all over for you.

Knock, Knock.   Who's there?
Abby.   Abby, who?
Abby birthday to you.

Knock, Knock. Who's there?
Butternut. Butternut, who?
Butternut let me in. My feet are muddy.

Knock, Knock. Who's there?
Dewey. Dewey, who?
Dewey have to go to school today?

Knock, Knock. Who's there?
Hook. Hook, who?
Hook cares?

Knock, Knock. Who's there?
Isabel. Isabel, who?
Isabel louder than a knock?

Knock, Knock. Who's there?
Boyd. Boyd, who?
Boydo you ask a lot of questions.

Knock, Knock. Who's there?
Candy. Candy, who?
Candy-magine why you'd want to know.

Knock, Knock. Who's there?
Emma. Emma, who?
Emma going to the store. Want to come along?

Knock, Knock. Who's there?
Sam. Sam, who?
Sam times you make me so mad!

Knock, Knock. Who's there?
Alcott. Alcott, who?
Alcott the grass if you'll cut the bushes.

Knock, Knock. Who's there?
Scold. Scold, who?
Scold outside, let me in!

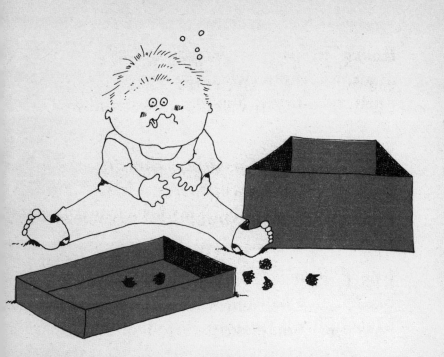

Knock, Knock.   Who's there?
Harriet.   Harriet, who?
Harriet a whole box of candy.
And now he has a stomachache!

Knock, Knock.   Who's there?
Bull.   Bull, who?
Bull down the shades. The sun is shining
in my eyes.

Knock, Knock.   Who's there?
Daniel.   Daniel, who?
Daniel so loud. I can hear you.

Knock, Knock.   Who's there?
Halibut.   Halibut, who?
Halibut letting me borrow a dollar?

Knock, Knock.   Who's there?
The force.   The force, who?
The force time I knocked, nobody answered!

Knock, Knock. Who's there?
Juan. Juan, who?
Juan, two, three, four.

Knock, Knock. Who's there?
Lena. Lena, who?
Lena little closer, and I'll whisper in your ear.

Knock, Knock. Who's there?
Mabel. Mabel, who?
Mabel I'll tell you, and mabel I won't.

Knock, Knock. Who's there?
Police. Police, who?
Police knock a little softer.

Knock, Knock. Who's there?
Henny. Henny, who?
Henny body wanna jump rope?

Knock, Knock.   Who's there?
Lion.   Lion, who?
Lion only gets me a spanking.

Knock, Knock.   Who's there?
Rita.   Rita, who?
Rita book and you might learn something.

Knock, Knock.   Who's there?
Sawyer.   Sawyer, who?
**Sawyer lights on, so thought I'd stop by
and say hello.**

Knock, Knock.   Who's there?
Tennis.   Tennis, who?
Tennis five plus five.

Knock, Knock.   Who's there?
Usher.   Usher, who?
Usher would like a piece of chocolate cake!

Knock, Knock.   Who's there?
Doris.   Doris, who?
Doris open, come on in.

Knock, Knock.   Who's there?
Fido.   Fido, who?
Fidon't you call me on Saturday?

Knock, Knock.   Who's there?
Hugo.   Hugo, who?
Hugo to the head of the class.

Knock, Knock.   Who's there?
Olive.   Olive, who?
Olive right down the street. Where do you live?

Knock, Knock.   Who's there?
Harris.   Harris, who?
Harris another name for a rabbit.

Knock, Knock.   Who's there?
Ice cream.   Ice cream, who?
Ice cream, you scream, we all scream for ice cream.

Knock, Knock.   Who's there?
Otto.   Otto, who?
Otto know if you don't.

Knock, Knock.   Who's there?
Paul.   Paul, who?
Paul over, buddy, you're driving too fast.

Knock, Knock.   Who's there?
Ringo.   Ringo, who?
Ringo round the collar.

Knock, Knock.   Who's there?
You.   You, who?
You-who to you, too!

Knock, Knock.   Who's there?
Russell.   Russell, who?
Russell up some vittles, pardner. I'm starved!

Knock, Knock.   Who's there?
Benny.   Benny, who?
Benny for your thoughts.

Knock, Knock.   Who's there?
Carmen.   Carmen, who?
Carmen over to my house!

Knock, Knock.   Who's there?
Gorilla.   Gorilla, who?
Gorilla my dreams, I love you.

Knock, Knock.   Who's there?
Cecil.   Cecil, who?
Cecil have music wherever she goes.

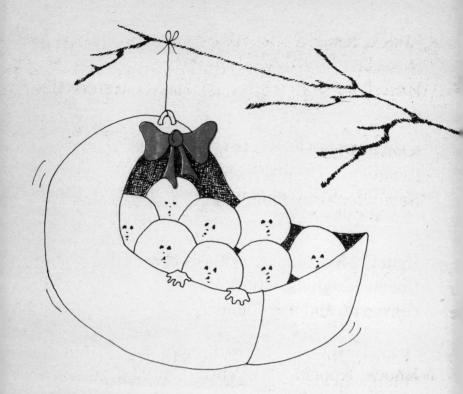

Knock, Knock.   Who's there?
Rocky.   Rocky, who?
Rocky-bye baby, in the treetop.

Knock, Knock.   Who's there?
Hyde.   Hyde, who?
Hyde like to tell you, but I can't!

Knock, Knock.   Who's there?
Juneau.   Juneau, who?
Juneau what time it is?

Knock, Knock.   Who's there?
Ron.   Ron, who?
Ron and get me a glass of water.

Knock, Knock.   Who's there?
Orange.   Orange, who?
Orange you glad I came over?

Knock, Knock. Who's there?
Boyer. Boyer, who?
Boyer a sight for sore eyes!

Knock, Knock. Who's there?
Dustin. Dustin, who?
**Dustin' and makin' my bed are two things
I don't like to do.**

Knock, Knock. Who's there?
Jess. Jess, who?
Jess you and me, kid.

Knock, Knock. Who's there?
Fiddlesticks. Fiddlesticks, who?
**The fiddlesticks if you don't put rosin
on the bow.**

Knock, Knock. Who's there?
Holt. Holt, who?
Holt up your hands. I gotcha covered!

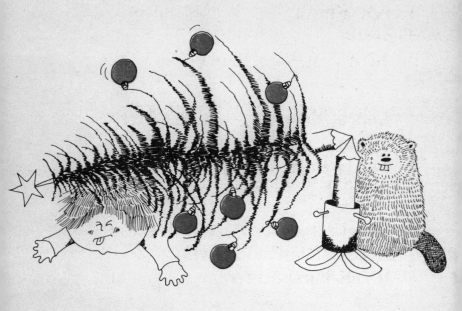

Knock, Knock.   Who's there?
Tim.   Tim, who?
Tim–ber!!

Knock, Knock.   Who's there?
Ivan.   Ivan, who?
Ivan to come in!

Knock, Knock.   Who's there?
Kent.   Kent, who?
Kent you see I'm too busy to talk to you?

Knock, Knock.   Who's there?
Max.   Max, who?
Max no difference to me!

Knock, Knock.   Who's there?
Roxanne.   Roxanne, who?
**Roxanne stones may break my bones,
but names can never hurt me.**

Knock, Knock. Who's there?
Justin. Justin, who?
Justin old friend here to see you.

Knock, Knock. Who's there?
Meyer. Meyer, who?
Meyer early. I'm not quite ready yet.

Knock, Knock. Who's there?
Rhoda. Rhoda, who?
Rhoda horse yesterday and fell off.

Knock, Knock. Who's there?
Wendy. Wendy, who?
Wendy you want to come out and play?

Knock, Knock. Who's there?
Heidi. Heidi, who?
Heidi-n here, they'll never find us!

Knock, Knock. Who's there?
Miya. Miya, who?
Miya have a nice pair of shoes!

Knock, Knock. Who's there?
Wade. Wade, who?
Wade and see!

Knock, Knock. Who's there?
Carson. Carson, who?
Carson the highway make lots of smog.

Knock, Knock. Who's there?
Ella. Ella, who?
Ella-mentary school is a grind.

Knock, Knock. Who's there?
Gwen. Gwen, who?
Gwen home, your mother's calling!

Knock, Knock.   Who's there?
Hominy.   Hominy, who?
Hominy times are you going to ask me?

Knock, Knock.   Who's there?
Ida.   Ida, who?
Ida wanna tell you.

Knock, Knock.   Who's there?
Lemmy.   Lemmy, who?
Lemmy a quarter, will you?

Knock, Knock.   Who's there?
Otis.   Otis, who?
Otis a beautiful day!

Knock, Knock.   Who's there?
Stan.   Stan, who?
Stan on your own two feet.

Knock, Knock.   Who's there?
Yukon.   Yukon, who?
Yukon lead a horse to water, but you can't make it drink!

Knock, Knock.   Who's there?
Owl.   Owl, who?
Owl never tell.

Knock, Knock.   Who's there?
Shelby.   Shelby, who?
Shelby comin' round the mountain when she comes!

Knock, Knock.   Who's there?
Wooden.   Wooden, who?
Wooden you like to know?

Knock, Knock.   Who's there?
Cashew.   Cashew, who?
Gesundheit!

Knock, Knock.   Who's there?
Eve.   Eve, who?
Eve you want me, just whistle.

Knock, Knock.   Who's there?
Francis.   Francis, who?
**Francis where the Statue of Liberty
comes from.**

Knock, Knock.   Who's there?
Philip.   Philip, who?
Philip my glass with another soda.

Knock, Knock.   Who's there?
Everett.   Everett, who?
Everett all the spinach on your plate?

Knock, Knock.   Who's there?
Who.   Who, who?
What are you, an owl?

Knock, Knock.   Who's there?
Burden.   Burden, who?
A burden the hand is worth two in the bush.

Knock, Knock.   Who's there?
Farm.   Farm, who?
Farm-e to know and you to find out.

Knock, Knock.   Who's there?
Ellis.   Ellis, who?
Ellis the 12th letter of the alphabet.

Knock, Knock.   Who's there?
Gopher.   Gopher, who?
Gopher a long walk, and don't come back!

Knock, Knock.   Who's there?
Rhett.   Rhett, who?
Rhett-y or not, here I come!

Knock, Knock.   Who's there?
Sarah.   Sarah, who?
Sarah doorbell around here? I'm tired
of knocking!

Knock, Knock.   Who's there?
Nanny.   Nanny, who?
Nanny your business!

Knock, Knock.   Who's there?
Eaton.   Eaton, who?
Eaton between meals is a no-no!

Knock, Knock.   Who's there?
Vera.   Vera, who?
Vera great team, aren't we?

Knock, Knock.   Who's there?
Doughnut.   Doughnut, who?
Doughnut count your chickens before
they're hatched.

Knock, Knock.   Who's there?
Pecan.   Pecan, who?
Pecan someone your own size!

Knock, Knock.   Who's there?
Winnie.   Winnie, who?
Winnie you gonna let me in?

Knock, Knock.   Who's there?
Sol.   Sol, who?
Sol-long, it's been good to see you.

Knock, Knock.   Who's there?
Thistle.   Thistle, who?
Thistle be the last knock-knock in the book.

Knock, Knock.   Who's there?
Les.   Les, who?
Les do some more knock-knocks!

This book is published by

PRICE/STERN/SLOAN
Publishers, Inc., Los Angeles

whose other splendid titles include literary classics as:

MAKE ME LAUGH ($1.50)

**HOW TO GET A TEENAGER
TO RUN AWAY FROM HOME ($1.75)**

WORLD'S WORST KNOCK KNOCK JOKES ($1.75)

WORLD'S WORST MORON JOKES ($1.75)

WORLD'S WORST RIDDLES ($1.75)

WORLD'S WORST ELEPHANT JOKES ($1.75)

WORLD'S WORST JOKES ($1.75)

and many, many more

They are available wherever books are sold, or may be
ordered directly from the publisher by sending check or money
order for the full amount of each title plus $1.00 for handling
and mailing. For a complete list of titles send a
stamped, self-addressed envelope to:

PRICE/STERN/SLOAN *Publishers, Inc.*
410 North La Cienega Boulevard, Los Angeles, California 90048